EVEN EAGLES
NEED A PUSH
THE POWER OF ENCOURAGEMENT

BY DAVID McNALLY AND MAC ANDERSON

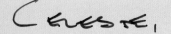

Celeste,

Keep Soar.on!

David McNally

Published by Simple Truths
1952 McDowell Road, Suite 205
Naperville, Illinois 60563

Toll Free 800-900-3427

Book Design: Vieceli Design Company, West Dundee, Illinois
Simple Truths is a registered trademark.
Printed and bound in the United States of America.

Editing by Stephanie Trannel
Photography by iStockphoto.com and © 2009 John Warden / AlaskaStock.com (page 10-11)
Illustration by Paul Turnbaugh Illustration

ISBN 978-1-60810-039-2

www.simpletruths.com

02 WOZ 09

TABLE OF CONTENTS

"You never know when
one kind act, or
one word of encouragement,
can change a life forever."

— *Zig Ziglar*

INTRODUCTION

The words on the opposite page were spoken by Zig Ziglar, and I couldn't agree more! I've seen the power of kindness and encouragement countless times; that's why I jumped at the chance to co-author this book with my friend, David McNally. I hope that reading a story about how kindness changed someone's life forever is enough to inspire you to offer your own encouragement. I think we all want to make a difference and there's no better way than to offer a shot of inspiration when someone really needs it.

We're starting this book by sharing McNally's beautiful story, about a mother eagle, called *The Push*. To me, it captures the essence of what this little book is all about. Enjoy!

To Life,

Mac Anderson
Founder, Simple Truths

THE
PUSH

by David McNally

The eagle gently coaxed her offspring toward the edge of the nest. Her heart quivered with conflicting emotions as she felt their resistance to her persistent nudging.

"Why does the thrill of soaring have to begin with the fear of falling?" she thought. This ageless question was still unanswered for her.

As in the tradition of the species, her nest was located high upon the shelf of a sheer rock face. Below there was nothing but air to support the wings of each child.

"Is it possible that this time it will not work?" she thought. Despite her fears the eagle knew it was time. Her parental mission was all but complete.

There remained one final task ... the push. The eagle drew courage from an innate wisdom. Until her children discovered their wings, there was no purpose for their lives.

Until they learned how to soar, they would fail to understand the privilege it was to have been born an eagle. The push was the greatest gift she had to offer. It was her supreme act of love.

And so, one by one, she pushed them and ...
THEY FLEW.

THE PUSH ...

Sometimes

WE NEED IT.

Sometimes

WE NEED TO GIVE IT.

It can be the greatest gift you ever give.
It will change a life forever.

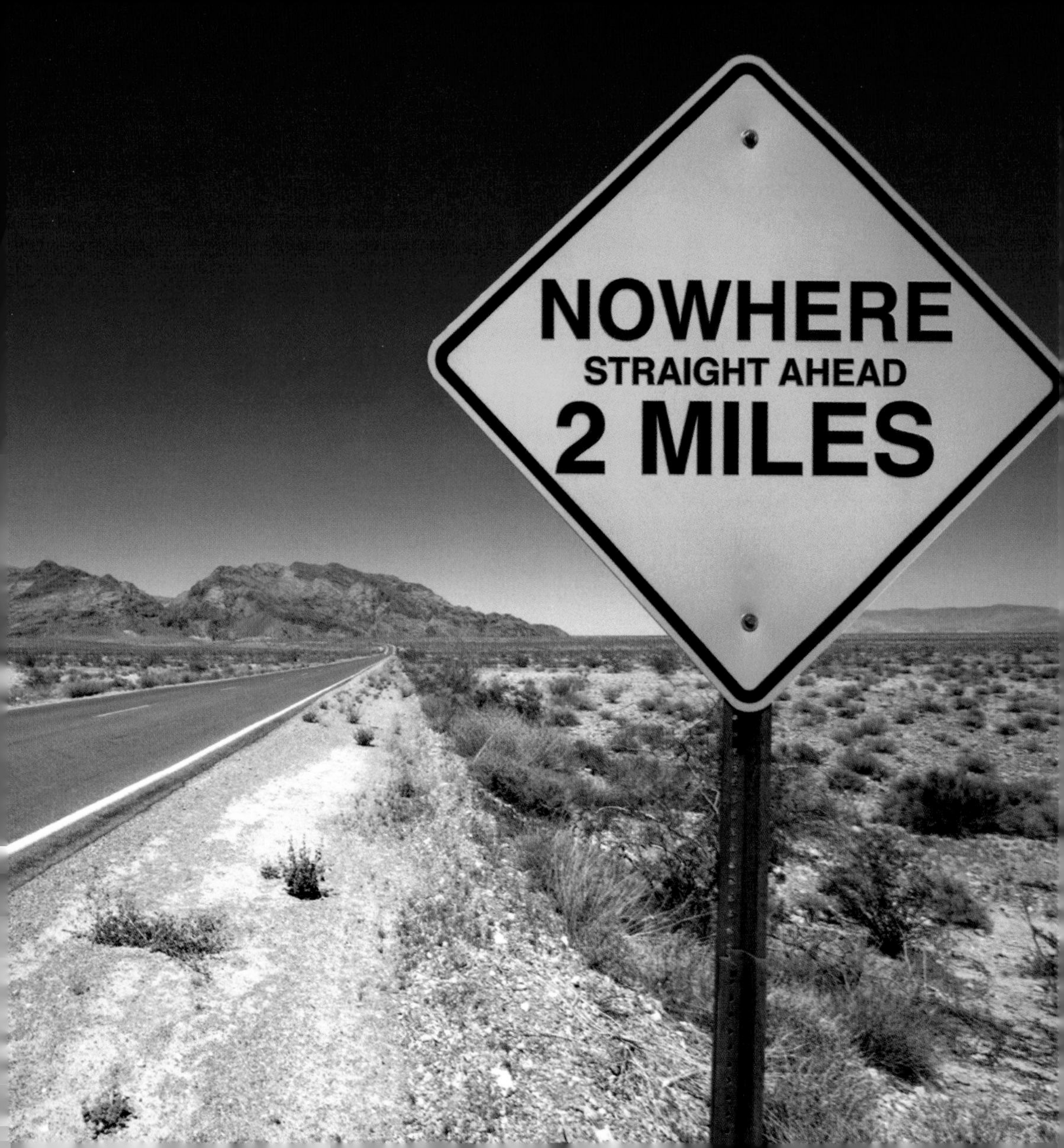
NOWHERE
STRAIGHT AHEAD
2 MILES

1

Don't Settle for Ordinary

by David McNally

Encouragement can come in many forms. Sometimes it is the courageous, honest words of a friend or loved one that help us make a course correction away from self-defeating and limiting behavior. Such words were spoken to me one cold and windy morning. Perhaps a little background might help.

As a young person I was very ambitious. Impatience, fueled by an intense desire to succeed, led me to forego college and start my first business straight out of high school. I was not suspicious or afraid of "get rich quick" schemes; on the contrary, I wanted to get rich, and the quicker, the better.

By my mid-twenties my drive had propelled me to a level of success that included fancy cars, a beautiful home, international travel, and Europe as my playground. All this was clear evidence that I had joined the ranks of those who had "made it."

At the age of twenty-eight my business failed. Having merged my whole identity with the business, when it disintegrated, so did I. Besides having nothing, I felt I was nothing. The downhill slide was slow, steady and painful. Convinced that I had blown the most wonderful opportunity life would ever present, I saw no promise in the future whatsoever.

I took refuge in late nights out with friends, which severely threatened my marriage. Ironically, it was my wife who rescued me.

One morning I came to the breakfast table nursing a king-sized hangover—not exactly a time when one is looking for advice! However, my receptiveness was of no concern to my wife, who was determined to confront me with the truth.

Quietly, slowly and succinctly, she uttered words that will be indelibly imprinted on my mind:

"DAVID, YOU ARE BECOMING SO ORDINARY."

Ordinary! Ordinary! The words seared my fuzzy brain and haunted me for the rest of the day. At my core I had long believed that there was no such thing as an ordinary human being. "What have you been doing?" I asked myself. "Two years ago you were on top of the world and now you have plunged to inconceivable depths."

Insight and learning comes only when one is open and ready. My wife's words had left me a vulnerable, yet willing, student. I immediately received what is known as a blinding glimpse of the obvious. So life had been unfair to me. So what? Had it not been unfair to millions of others? Had many of them not faced far worse circumstances? Had they accepted defeat?

My reaction for two years had been to be a victim and to remain a victim. My behavior of blaming, excuse making and finger pointing was getting me nowhere. The guidepost to a positive future flashed like a neon sign: personal responsibility. It was a road that I knew would not be easy, but upon which I was ready to embark without the slightest hesitation.

Since that morning, I have built a successful new business, written several books, produced films, and been a guest speaker at conferences all over the world. There has been no greater learning for me than within the events and circumstances of our lives is the wisdom upon which to build our futures.

My life has taught me that mistakes don't matter, failure doesn't matter. What matters is that we continue to move forward and grow from our experiences. Hal Prince, the famous Broadway producer, said: **"Anyone who hasn't had a failure is an amateur."**

My wife, Jo, has passed away. Her words from many years ago, spoken with candor yet great love, are my ongoing encouragement to settle for nothing less than the extraordinary.

2

Where Do I Go From Here?

by Mac Anderson

The year was 1998. It had been difficult to say the least. The business (Successories) was struggling and I had just been diagnosed with prostate cancer. As we all know, the "c word" gets our attention.

I was trying to re-evaluate my life and decide, "Where do I go from here?" After some real soul searching, I decided to hire Gary Rovansek to run the day-to-day at Successories so I could step down into an advisory role. I had been an entrepreneur for 25 years, fighting many battles along the way ... but I was yearning to move in a different direction. Don't get me wrong, I loved doing what I was doing, but cancer always makes you re-evaluate your priorities in life. I wanted to relax and think for a while about plan B.

For almost two years, I did just that. I'm thankful to say that after treatment my cancer was in remission. Those two years felt wonderful! It gave me the opportunity to unclutter my brain and re-visit some of the good things I had done and some of the mistakes I had made. But even though my "semi-retirement" felt good, I knew I wasn't being fulfilled. At the same time, my time off caused me to ask myself some questions: "Am I ready to fight more battles? **What can I do to fuel my passion to reinforce the positive in the world? Is it possible I could fail? Do I want to take that risk?**"

All of these thoughts and others were causing me to sit on the "fence of indecision." It didn't feel good, but to be perfectly honest, at this point in my life, I didn't have the courage to take action. I think we've all been there.

I got a call from Rich Rush, who was our VP of Production at Successories. Rich said, "Mac, I haven't talked with you in a while and I'd love to buy you lunch."

The following week we got together, and during lunch Rich asked the question, "Mac, what do you plan to do with the rest of your life?" Not knowing exactly what to say, I said, "I might just sit it out and relax a bit." I'll never forget his face when he looked up and said, "**You can't do that! You've got too much to say that could make a difference in the lives of too many people. You'll be cheating yourself and many others if you don't use the talent God has given you.**"

After lunch, I found myself doing a lot of thinking about what Rich had said, and I knew I couldn't just sit on the sidelines and let my life go by without giving my passion another shot.

I've often thought, without that conversation, would there be a Simple Truths today? Would I have had the opportunity to write the books that I've written, and would I have had the honor to speak to hundreds of corporate audiences? I don't know for sure, but I think the answer would be no.

For some reason that day those words of encouragement turned the switch from "off" to "on" and shoved me right off the fence onto a new path that I love. In fact, I can say without a doubt, these years have been the most rewarding of my life.

Just knowing what that day did for me is one of the reasons that I readily embraced the chance to co-author this book with my friend, David McNally.

> ## "THE DOORS WE OPEN AND CLOSE EACH DAY DECIDE THE LIVES WE LIVE."
>
> — *Flora Whittemore*

3

The Power of a NOTE

by Fred Bauer

On my first job as sports editor for the *Montpelier* (Ohio) *Leader Enterprise*, I didn't get a lot of fan mail, so I was intrigued by a letter plopped on my desk one morning. The envelope bore the logo of the closest big-city paper, the *Toledo Blade*.

When I opened it, I read:

"Sweet piece of writing on the Tigers. Keep up the good work."

It was signed by Don Wolfe, the sports editor. Because I was a teenager (being paid the grand total of 15 cents a column inch), his words could not have been more exhilarating. I kept the letter in my desk drawer until it got rag-eared. Whenever I doubted I had the right stuff to be a writer, I would reread Don's note and walk on air again.

Later, when I got to know him, I learned that Don made a habit of jotting a quick, encouraging word to people in all walks of life. **"When I make others feel good about themselves,"** he told me, **"I feel good, too."**

Why are upbeat note writers in such short supply? My guess is that many who shy away from the practice are too self-conscious. They are afraid they will be misunderstood, sound corny or fawning. Also, writing takes time and it is far easier to pick up the phone. The drawback with phone calls, of course, is that they do not last. A note attaches more importance to our well-wishing. It is a matter of record, and our words can be read more than once, savored, and treasured.

What does it take to write notes that lift spirits and warm hearts? Perhaps just a desire and a willingness to express our appreciation. The most successful practitioners write notes that are short on verbiage and long on empathy; sincere, short, specific, and usually spontaneous in nature.

It is difficult to be spontaneous, however, when you have to hunt for letter writing materials; so, keep paper, envelopes, and stamps close at hand, even when you travel. Fancy stationery is not necessary; it's the thought that counts.

So, who around you deserves a note of thanks or approval? A neighbor, your librarian, a relative, your mayor, your mate, a teacher, or doctor? You do not need to be poetic. If you need a reason, look for a milestone, the anniversary of a special event you shared, a birthday, or holiday, and do not constrain your praise. Superlatives such as: "greatest," "smartest," "prettiest" make us all feel good. Even if your plaudits run a little ahead of reality, remember that expectations are often the parents of dreams fulfilled.

Today, I received a warm, complimentary letter from my old boss and mentor, Norman Vincent Peale. He once told me that the purpose of writing inspirational notes (he is the best three-sentence letter writer I have ever known) is simply **"to build others up because there are too many people in the demolition business today."**

His little note to me was full of uplifting phrases, and it sent me to my typewriter to compose a few overdue letters of my own. I don't know if they will make anybody else's day, but they made mine. As my friend Don Wolfe said, "Making others feel good about themselves makes me feel good, too."

4

A Teacher's Legacy

by Wayne Dyer

I was inspired by Mrs. Olive Fletcher. In 1956, I was taking biology for the second time at Denby High School in Detroit. I'd failed the class the previous year because of my own stubbornness: **I'd refused to complete a leaf collection, which my then 15-year-old self perceived to be an absurd requirement.**

At that time, my mother was divorcing my alcoholic step-father, and I was working in a local grocery store every evening during the week and all day on Saturday and Sunday. My instructor for this second foray into biology was Mrs. Fletcher, and she was the very first teacher I encountered who seemed to care about me personally. For example, she was there for me after school, called my home to see if I was okay during the tumultuousness (including frequent fights and other unpleasantness) taking place at the time, and allowed me to put my head down and sleep during study periods when I'd completed my assignments. She also encouraged me to tutor other students because she recognized something in me that I'd never heard a teacher say before: She told me that I was brilliant and had a mind that could take me wherever I wanted to go.

This incredible person even invited me to go bowling with her and her husband. Before I met Mrs. Fletcher, I'd never imagined that teachers were actually human, let alone went bowling. She was the first "authority figure" who welcomed my questioning and tolerated my sometimes disruptive behavior. She showed me that I was worthy of being loved by someone in a position of authority.

Thanks to Mrs. Fletcher's inspiration, I went from a failing grade the previous year to an A. I wanted to excel just for her because she had so much faith in me. Now, exactly a half century later, Mrs. Olive Fletcher still stands out as the one individual in all of my school years who turned the direction of my life from fighting the system to being able to choose to fit in without having to give in.

(Excerpted from Inspiration Your Ultimate Calling*)*

"THE BEST WAY TO INSPIRE PEOPLE TO SUPERIOR PERFORMANCE IS TO CONVINCE THEM BY EVERYTHING YOU DO AND BY YOUR EVERYDAY ATTITUDE THAT YOU ARE WHOLEHEARTEDLY SUPPORTING THEM."

— *Harold S. Geneen*

Go back to
school get
MBA!

5

Why Can't YOU?

by Ellen Parlapiano

Brigitte Payne Cogswell's busy schedule hangs front and center of the fridge in her New Haven, Connecticut, kitchen. Even a cursory glance at her calendar reveals that there's rarely a spare minute. Mornings and early afternoons are booked solid with appointments for onsite training at local schools, hospitals and municipal organizations—all part of her job as the owner of a diversity consulting firm called *Success by Design*. Late afternoons and evenings are for shuttling her two daughters, Agape, 11, and Destiny, 8, to and from a jam-packed roster of activities. Yet, Brigitte, 47, still manages to block out every Monday from 2:30 p.m. to 8:30 p.m. to attend classes toward her MBA, the degree she's wanted to earn ever since she was in her 20s.

Brigitte credits her mother for teaching her that it's never too late to go back to school. *"When I was a teenager, my mom earned her BA at the age of 48 and fulfilled her dream of becoming a social worker. She told me that I must go beyond what she achieved."*

So right after high school, Brigitte headed to Connecticut College in New London. After graduating with a bachelor's degree in human relations, she started working as a management trainee at a bank to get her career under way, intending to take MBA classes at night. Though she stuck to the plan by enrolling in grad school in the early 1990s, an intimidating statistics course did her in, and she quit halfway through her semester. She figured she'd give it another try someday.

Then came one summer afternoon in 2006, when a brochure for the University of New Haven's Executive MBA program arrived in the mail.

"Boy, I would love to do that," Brigitte remembers saying as she looked over the pamphlet with Agape, then 9. *"Why can't you?"* asked Agape. It was just the nudge Brigitte needed. "I was worried about having enough money, but Agape kept saying,

"IF THIS IS SOMETHING YOU WANT, YOU SHOULD GO FOR IT, MOM."

Brigitte had always taught her girls that you can't put a price on education, and now was her chance to prove it.

The girls are reveling in their new role as teaching assistants. Agape helps Brigitte prepare her Powerpoint presentations, Destiny organizes Mom's folder. Brigitte is confident her daughters' enthusiasm for learning will endure throughout their lives. "Just as I went above and beyond what my mother accomplished in terms of education, I want them to surpass me." So far, it looks like the girls plan to do just that. Even in casual conversation both often talk about college, and Agape already has a loftier goal: medical school.

(Excerpted from "Live and Learn," Family Circle Magazine, June 2008.)

6

Show Business, MAYBE?

In his autobiography, *Leading With My Chin*, former Tonight Show host Jay Leno recounts his struggles in school and how one teacher got him thinking about his life's direction.

Another teacher who made a huge impression was Mr. Walsh. For whatever reason, he was always assigned to oversee detention duty in the library. And since I was always in detention, we'd sit together almost every day. Mr. Walsh was one of those guys who would laugh at anything. Tell him the simplest joke and he'd break up. Everything was hilarious to this man. So I'd have new stories for him all the time. One day he said to me,

"WHY DON'T YOU THINK ABOUT GOING INTO SHOW BUSINESS?"

This was a revelation. The idea never even occurred to me. I didn't know anybody in show business. The closest thing was an eighth-grade teacher who did magic tricks at student assemblies. And that was unbelievable! Someone we knew who could actually entertain people! When you grow up in a small town like Andover, MA, show business is the furthest thing from being a career option.

But Mr. Walsh's words ignited something in me. I began telling people that I wanted to one day become a comedian.

Dubbed by media and his peers as the "Hardest-Working Man in Show Business," Jay performed everywhere he could, from college campuses to Carnegie Hall to Las Vegas. He always wanted to host The Tonight Show and he achieved that goal in 1992, when he replaced late-night TV legend Johnny Carson. Jay shared his unique wit with The Tonight Show audience for 17 years, before launching a new prime-time show in 2009.

"LIFE IS NOT MADE UP OF **GREAT SACRIFICES AND DUTIES** BUT OF LITTLE THINGS: IN WHICH **SMILES AND KINDNESS** GIVEN HABITUALLY ARE WHAT WIN AND PRESERVE THE HEART AND SECURE COMFORT."

— *Sir Humphry Davy*

7

A Life-Changing
EXPERIENCE

We touch the lives of others in ways we often never know. People some-times come into our personal world for fleeting moments and can leave us forever changed. We have more power to create or to destroy than we can imagine. We can leave things or individuals better or worse than we found them. A look, a word, a gesture has tremendous impact and frequently we blither along blind to the effect every communication wields.

I learned this in a powerful way:

It was a rainy, humid day: the mother of all bad hair days. I was riding on a bus downtown to go to work. Everyone was wilting. I was sitting next to a man in a business suit and didn't pay him much attention until we both got off at the same stop and walked to the same newsstand to get a morning paper.

The man running the stand was obviously among those having a bad day. He was rude, abrupt and unsmiling as we purchased our papers, which served to add only more gloom to my day. The businessman caught my eye and smiled. He then proceeded to smile even more brightly, thank the newsstand proprietor for the paper and for being open on such a morning to make sure we were able to get our papers. In short, he expressed his appreciation for something most of us would take for granted.

The man running the newsstand responded only with a grunt and a sour expression. The businessman then pleasantly wished him a pleasant day.

As we turned away, I asked this man why he had continued to be pleasant to the newsman when he obviously didn't care about and didn't respond to his expression of appreciation and friendliness. The businessman grinned at me and said,

> "WHY WOULD I LET SOMEONE ELSE CONTROL WHAT I SAY AND WHAT I FEEL OR WHAT KIND OF DAY I'M GOING TO HAVE?"

I never saw the businessman again, even though I looked for him on the bus on other days. He appeared briefly in my life and disappeared just as quickly. I don't even remember what he looked like. But I've never forgotten the words he said, or the way his smile seemed like a shaft of light on a gloomy day.

That was a good 25 years ago, but the impact this had on my life has lasted. I never had a chance to thank him personally, but the way in which I choose to look at life as a result of those words is his legacy to me and my thanks to him.

Our interactions with the people we encounter can impact at least the next five people they encounter. A smile and words of simple appreciation multiply themselves geometrically.

We cannot control people and situations that come to us, but we can

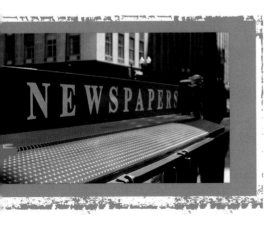

always control our responses to them. In each of our decisions lies our power to make a positive difference. It's something anyone and everyone can do.

(Story submitted by Gail Pursell Elliott. Gail is President of Innovations: Training With Can-Do Attitude.)

8

Anytime You
SHOW UP

I've always loved jazz, partly because its essence depends on improvisation—musicians completely tuned into each other responding with original yet harmonious replies.

One of the most gifted improvisers around is jazz violinist Zach Brock. Barely in his 30s, the jazz world was already beyond a buzz and edging toward a roar. A *Chicago Tribune* review applauded his "rising stature as the rare jazz fiddler with something significant to say."

Zach's life was—and still is—pretty great. But despite his enormous gift, Zach once fiddled around with abandoning music. That's when Myron Kartman, Zach's music professor at Northwestern University, stepped up with his own brilliant improvisation.

Here's Zach Brock's story:

Two months into his sophomore year at Northwestern, Zach was crushed by a car. "It was October 30th, 1993. I was riding my bike and was the victim of a hit and run accident," he recalls. "My femur came out the side of my pants, my eye socket was broken, my kneecap was smashed into eight pieces, my tibia and fibula were bent. This man heard the crash from inside his house. He called an ambulance and saved my life."

Police eventually arrested the hit-and-run driver, but Zach's path spiraled downward. Bed-bound for six months, he dropped out of school and moved back home. It took years of physical therapy and multiple surgeries before he could walk without serious pain. "I played violin as soon as I could," Zach says. "Somehow, nothing happened to my back or hands, so at points during my recovery, sitting in a chair and playing was all I could do. Everything else was pain and misery. I was crippled with depression. Even when I got better physically, I got sicker

and sicker mentally. I became a puny, fragile, 130-pound mess. But, I could still play violin."

At one point, Zach tried going back to school, but it was too hard to navigate the campus and he was too depressed to focus. He dropped out again. "I didn't want to go home," Zach explains. "My parents were frustrated and scared for me, and I was really messed up. All we did was fight. So I moved into an apartment near the North-western campus. Myron Kartman told me he'd still give me lessons anytime I could show up. Myron taught me for three years without taking a cent. It's not like I was the darling of the studio. He's just that kind of guy."

(*Excerpted from* Strings *magazine.*)

Those words "anytime I could show up" meant that Kartman's door remained always and unconditionally open. Zach's teacher's words may not have been the common encouragement of "you can do it," but they were the perfect words, giving Zach exactly what he needed: time to heal. And eventually Zach's wonderful spirit responded ... with an original yet harmonious reply.

9

The Remarkable Journey of
DOCTOR Q

Alfredo Quinones-Hinojosa grew up in Mexico. Arriving in the U.S. as an illegal migrant farm worker in 1987 at the age of 19, he spoke no English and had less than $5 in his pocket. Today, Dr. Quinones – or Dr. Q as he is called by his colleagues – is a neurosurgeon, Assistant Professor of Neurosurgery and Oncology and Director of the Brain Tumor Surgery Program at Hopkins Bayview.

$e = mc^2$

His first job in America was pulling weeds in tomato and cotton fields in California's San Joaquin Valley. But, Quinones' burning desire to achieve led him to the San Joaquin Delta Community College in Stockton, Calif., where he attended classes and led literacy and statistics workshops for fellow immigrants. He later attended the University of California at Berkeley, where he served as a lab assistant and a calculus and physics tutor for students from low-income backgrounds.

Inspired by the example of his grandmother, a curandera—village healer back home in Mexico—and by his own desire to connect with people in a deep way, Quinones decided while at Berkeley to pursue a career in medicine. He had set his sights on less competitive medical schools when his mentor, an administrator who ran a Hispanic Center of Excellence, intervened.

"When he saw my CV and my grades, the first thing that came out of his mouth, in a thick Mexican accent, was, 'Oh amigo, with these grades, you can easily get to Harvard.' I thought this guy was clearly living la vida loca."

It was a story he told in 1999 when he delivered the commencement address at Harvard Medical School, where he graduated cum laude and became an American citizen.

After Harvard, he completed his residency in neurosurgery at the University of California at San Francisco. Today, his lab at Hopkins Bayview is one of the most racially and ethnically diverse on campus—a consequence of his belief that *"as you go up in life, you should always look back and help the people behind you."*

When Quinones delivered a talk at the University of Guadalajara, it was the first time he'd been back to Mexico. "I left a peasant; I came back a professor," he says.

His own ascent was the result of tremendous energy, ambition, determination and especially, he says, *the influence of mentors.*

"PEOPLE HAVE GIVEN ME SO MUCH. NOW I AM TRYING TO GIVE BACK AS MUCH AS I CAN."

(Excerpted from Dome, the publication of Johns Hopkins Medicine Family.)

10

A LESSON in Love

by Colleen Sell

When mother of four Susan Farr-Fahncke decides to take her children to a bowling alley on an outing, she is inspired by a "bowling alley hero."

The "I wants" and "I cants," the fidgeting and teasing, and the she-nanigans and bickering were quickly escalating. I was irritated with my two-year-old for repeatedly taking out his hearing aids and having to constantly chase after and retrieve him. I didn't take my eyes off my seven and thirteen-year-olds either; they required almost as much supervision as my toddler. At the moment, they were "bugging" each other, and I could feel a brawl coming on. I was grumbling shamelessly to myself and thinking that "family time" wasn't all it was cracked up to be.

Then I saw a father two lanes over with his two children—both were in wheelchairs.

I looked at my squabbling kids and back to his. His children had no motor control; they couldn't even hold the bowling ball. At the moment, mine were threatening to throw balls at each other.

I watched with amazement as the man patiently set up the special ramp used for disabled bowlers. I'd never realized before what a significant obstacle that step down into the bowling alley could be in a wheelchair. I'd never thought about how you could bowl if you had no control over your arms. My greatest bowling instruction challenge–teaching my child how to throw the bowling ball without pitching himself down the lane–paled in comparison. I watched in stunned admiration as the man placed an elevated apparatus, like a ski jump with runners, at the front of the lane each time it was one of his children's turns to bowl. He'd position the bowling ball at the top of the slope, gently place the child's hand on the ball, and discretely add a little "umph" to the push that sent it rolling down the alley.

To each child he spoke very softly, bending down to their eye level, gently instructing, encouraging, and cheering, never losing patience or resenting the effort it took to help them bowl. He

didn't seem to mind. In fact, he was genuinely having a blast and his eyes sparkled with love.

What in heaven was I doing, fretting and complaining, unable to enjoy a good time with my children? Four rambunctious children, one with impaired hearing, was not a huge burden in the grand scheme of things.

This man had made an afternoon of bowling into a magical day, and he was enjoying and cherishing every moment–in sharp contrast to the attitude with which I had approached this outing.

I wish I had the guts to go up to him and say what I was thinking, "I think you are an incredible person, and your kids are angels, and you impress and inspire me." But he left.

"If you're out there, man from the bowling alley, thank you for your shining example. Thank you for reminding me to love my children a little more. Thank you for your humble lesson in love. You are a hero."

(Excerpted from A Cup of Comfort.*)*

BOWLING

11

Getting Fired ... UP!

In his commencement speech at Stanford University in 2005, Steve Jobs, one of the co-founders of Apple Computer and founder of Pixar Studios, shared how getting fired from the company he started brought him to a new creative level:

I WAS LUCKY—I FOUND WHAT I LOVED TO DO EARLY IN LIFE. Woz (Steve Wozniak) and I started Apple in my parents' garage when I was 20. We worked hard, and in 10 years Apple had grown from just the two of us in a garage into a $2 billion company with over 4,000 employees. We had just released our finest creation—the Macintosh—a year earlier, and I had just turned 30. And then I got fired. How can you get fired from a company you started? Well, as Apple grew we hired someone who I thought was very talented to run the company with me, and for the first year or so things went well. But then our visions of the future began to diverge and eventually we had a falling out. When we did, our Board of Directors sided with him. So at 30 I was out, and very publicly out. *What had been the focus of my entire adult life was gone, and it was devastating.*

I really didn't know what to do for a few months. I felt that I had let the previous generation of entrepreneurs down—that I had dropped the baton as it was being passed to me. I was a very public failure, and I even thought about running away from the valley. But something slowly began to dawn on me—I still loved what I did. The turn of events at Apple had not changed that one bit. I had been rejected, but I was still in love. And so I decided to start over.

I didn't see it then, but it turned out that getting fired from Apple was the best thing that could have ever happened to me. The heaviness of being successful was replaced by the lightness of

being a beginner again, although less sure about everything. It freed me to enter one of the most creative periods of my life.

During the next five years, I started a company named NeXT, another company named Pixar, and fell in love with an amazing woman who would become my wife. Pixar went on to create the world's first computer animated *feature film,* Toy Story, *and is now the most successful animation studio in the world. In a remarkable turn of events, Apple bought NeXT, I returned to Apple, and the technology we developed at NeXT is at the heart of Apple's current renaissance.*

I'm pretty sure none of this would have happened if I hadn't been fired from Apple. It was awful tasting medicine, but I guess the patient needed it. Sometimes life hits you in the head with a brick. Don't lose faith. I'm convinced that the only thing that kept me going was that I loved what I did. Your work is going to fill a large part of your life, and the only way to be truly satisfied is to do what you believe is great work.

THE CIRCUMSTANCES OF OUR LIVES HAVE AS MUCH POWER AS
WE CHOOSE
TO GIVE THEM.

— David McNally

12

He Had the Real "MEDICINE" I Needed

by Amy Jones

I ventured down the unfamiliar pathway to the doctor's office. A bad cold forced me to seek the appointment, and I deliberately chose a doctor I had never seen before. It was much easier to face strangers than friends.

My life had come to an abrupt halt a few months earlier. The man I was married to chose to walk away from the life he knew. He suddenly disappeared, abandoning everything in his life, including me. He left messages at his work, for his family, and at our home that he was taking his life in "a different direction." In spite of all efforts, including filing a national missing persons report, he could not be found. And over the years that followed, I realized that I would never see him again.

I felt I had to deal with the message in silence. A pattern of secrecy within my marriage led me to fear authenticity and I desperately try to hide the situation. This choice left me feeling totally alone and only increased my feelings of abandonment. Therefore, when I sought out medical attention for my minor health concern, I wanted to find a doctor who didn't know me.

The stranger in the white lab jacket had never seen me before, and that's exactly the way I wanted it.

> **"Just tell me what's wrong, give me medication, and I'll be out of here,"** I thought as I entered his office. I did not know I would find the real "medicine" I needed from a caring doctor who stepped outside the usual bounds of his profession to point the way toward healing.

My throat hurt, but the intense pain I felt was much deeper than that. This must have been obvious to Dr. LeCroy as he questioned me about my physical condition. Gently he probed, trying to determine exactly what was wrong. Suddenly I began crying and pouring my heart out to him, something I had not done with anyone. He listened; but more than that, because of something he experienced in his own childhood, he understood! He gave me many words of encouragement, but his last words were the most important, the ones I will never forget.

He took me by the shoulders and looked straight into my eyes. "Hold on to God through this, Amy. If you hold on to God you will look back in five years and be amazed at what He has done in your life!" Five years seemed like an eternity, and I certainly couldn't imagine what life would be like by then! He handed me a prescription and sent me on my way. After I got in my car, I read the scrawled notation on the prescription slip. It simply read "Jer. 29:11." I recognized it as a verse from the Bible, but I did not know what the verse said or why Dr. LeCroy had written it.

I rushed home and into my bedroom, grabbed my Bible, and turned to the 29th chapter of the book of Jeremiah. And there was my "prescription!" "For I know the plans I have for you," declares the Lord, "plans to prosper you and not to harm you, plans to give you hope and a future." That was exactly what I didn't have in my life but so desperately needed: hope, no harm, a future, and a plan! As I read the verse over and over, I realized it addressed everything that was wrong with me. Anything and everything could be taken from me in an instant, but God and His Word would still be there. Jeremiah 29:11 became my Life Verse.

As I tried to figure out how to pick up the shattered pieces of my hopes and dreams, I clung to those promises found in my "prescription." With the words of Jeremiah 29:11 guiding me, I gave my entire life and future over to God. Two things were strongly impressed upon me: go back and finish college and use what I had been through to help others. I knew this could only come from God because I did not want to share my story, and I did not like going to school!

I encountered many obstacles as I tried to re-enter college. Nothing seemed to work until I discovered Dallas Baptist University. Peace filled me as I drove up the hill to the university's campus. **As I walked into the informational meeting, the facilitator was beginning with a video about the school. Looking up I saw a royal blue screen displaying the school's foundational verse, Jeremiah 29:11! I knew then I was where I was supposed to be.**

In the months that followed, I contemplated how to use what I'd been through to help others. I had always turned to my dad for advice, but he had lost his battle to cancer the year before my life began to fall apart. So I sought out his hero, Zig Ziglar, a man who was known for helping so many people. To my astonishment, I found that his office was only 45 minutes away from where I lived. I prepared my resume,

hoping that I could work in his office while observing how to use life experiences to help others. With directions in hand, I drove to his office, walked in the front door, and soon found myself speaking to the Human Resources Director. When I told him I wanted to learn to share my story with others, maybe in ten or fifteen years, he asked me to share it at their company devotions on the following Monday!

Monday came and I stood before Zig Ziglar and his entire team, pouring out my heart. What I thought would be a one-time chance to share my story became an opportunity of a lifetime as Mr. Ziglar launched my national speaking career within a few short weeks. Who would have thought my second speaking engagement would be in front of a sold-out crowd of 7,500 people alongside Zig Ziglar and six other famous presenters? Since that time I have spoken to over 500,000 people and shared the platform not only with Zig Ziglar but also with speakers and leaders such as Rudy Giuliani, Larry King, General Colin Powell, Suze Orman, Brian Tracy, and Tom Hopkins.

What an incredible ride! In 2005 someone asked me, "When are you going to complete your master's degree?" "May 12th," I said. Then it hit me. Dr. LeCroy told me I would look back in five years and be amazed at what God could do. That was exactly five years from the day my life fell apart!

13

You Can Always COME HOME

by Tim Schaefer

When I was in my early twenties, I moved away from my home state of Wisconsin to attend graduate school. I chose to go to the University of Arizona in Tucson and flew to the campus, sight-unseen. Upon landing in early June, I was shocked by the lack of green and the intense desert heat. After less than two days in that environment, I called my parents to question whether I had made the right choice and to announce that I was seriously considering coming home. My father, in a calm and supportive voice, indicated that I always had a choice. I could always come home and be welcome there.

We've discussed this moment several times since. We both knew that I wouldn't come home at the time, it was knowing that I had that option that allowed me to continue. I have been able to venture on to marriage, persevere through several challenging job situations, and endure my wife's severe health concerns during the birth of our only child by knowing that I can always "come home." **My father's encouraging words remain with me and I have used the phrase in special situations when others need to know that someone cares and they do have an option.**

WHETHER "HOME" IS EARTHLY,
SPIRITUAL, OR SOME SENSE OF CALM,
KNOWING THAT WE CAN COME
"HOME" IF NEEDED CAN BE JUST
ENOUGH TO HELP US ON OUR WAY.
IT REMINDS ME, IN A WAY, OF THE
PRODIGAL SON WHO FOUND COMFORT
AND LOVE UPON RETURNING HOME.
WHILE WE DON'T HAVE TO STRAY AND
HIT BOTTOM IN LIFE, IT IS GOOD TO
KNOW THAT WE CAN WANDER AND
EXHAUST LIFE'S TRIALS AND JOURNEYS
AND YET HAVE SOME HOME BASE
WHERE LOVE, SUPPORT, COMFORT
AND CALM EXISTS.

Your Dreams
NEXT EXIT ↗

14

Forgotten Your Dreams?

by Jack Canfield and Gay Hendricks

After a change in head coaches at the University of South Carolina earlier in his career, Lou Holtz, then a defensive coach, found himself unemployed.

"I was unemployed for over a month, a long time for someone like me who had worked since he was nine; I felt very defeated. Our savings account was down to four figures: around $10.95. With a growing family to support, I was feeling pressure. It would have been an unbearable period, if not for my wife. She could not have been more supportive or encouraging. Beth never complained. She went to work as an x-ray technician to help keep us in groceries. She also brought me the motivational book, The Magic of Thinking Big, *by David Schwartz, hoping it would help me feel less depressed.*

In his chapter on goals, Schwartz writes that anyone who is bored by life has probably forgotten his or her dreams. He invites readers to get back in touch with them. As a first step, we are asked to list all the things we have ever wanted to accomplish. I had a lot of time on my hands, so I took out a pencil and paper and divided my list into five categories:

1. AS A HUSBAND/FATHER
2. SPIRITUALLY
3. PROFESSIONALLY
4. FINANCIALLY
5. SIMPLY FOR EXCITEMENT

It was in the fifth category that I let my imagination run wild. Here are some of the things I included:

Things TO DO ...

1. Jump out of an airplane

2. Land a jet fighter on an aircraft carrier

3. Travel the ocean in a submarine

4. Go white–water rafting on the Snake River at Hells Canyon

5. Be on the Tonight Show, starring Johnny Carson

6. Attend a White House dinner with the President

7. Meet the Pope

8. Go on an African safari

9. Become a scratch golfer and play the top 50 golf courses in the world

10. Run with the bulls in Pamplona (provided I was matched with a much slower person)

And on it went. I had 107 goals on my original list. Suddenly, I was looking at my life differently and was excited about the future. When I told Beth that I was determined we do all of them, she said, "Gee, that's great honey, but why don't you add 'I want to find a job.'" Good note—the list expanded to 108.

So far, we've managed to achieve 102 of those dreams—including dining at the White House and meeting the Pope. We're still working on the others. From the moment I made that list, we became participants, rather than spectators, in our life. You do the same and you'll find you don't want to spend so much time sleeping; you'll be afraid you might miss something!

(Excerpted from You Gotta Read This Book.*)*

15

Spring Into ACTION!

by Susan Zimmerman

Isn't spring an invigorating season? Every year it seems like many of us have budding experiences in this rejuvenating time of year. New elements are bursting forth, just like the beautiful buds blossoming into their next life phase.

I especially remember one spring when my children were young. I was at home with my 4-year-old daughter and 2-year-old son. I noticed my daughter, Katie, was particularly quiet so I peeked around the corner to see why. She was sitting about halfway up the steps holding one of her shoes. We'd worked on tying a bow earlier that week. Now she was intently making loops on the little shoe strings, absolutely determined to tie a bow on her own.

Despite her focused labor, the strings weren't cooperating. **Persistently, she kept starting over, and over, and over.** The birth of a bow surely had to come soon! I was amazed at her patience. But suddenly she'd had it. As she stood and sent the shoe hurling across the full length of the living room, she simultaneously screamed and began sobbing.

Something told me to stay out of sight, to wait and watch. Her crying peaked, then waned and stopped. She sat silently for a few more seconds. Then she arose and walked calmly over to the shoe and picked it up. With utter resolve she returned to the step and resumed her effort. Shortly thereafter, a beautiful bouncing bow was born! We rejoiced with great celebration.

This story is one of the miracles in my life.

My daughter's feat was not heroic, but to me her perseverance was. For you see, that spring I felt dead. No buds, no blossoms. I was suddenly and unexpectedly single. As a teacher on an extended maternity leave, the jobs I sought were non-existent. Fear ruled my being. That is, until a little flying shoe was retrieved and pampered by its precious pitcher.

Hope poured into my soul. **Seemingly endless amounts of courage and creativity burst forth like buds blossoming in a fast motion film.** Metaphorically, my "untied shoe" was money. It was up to me alone to financially support my family, but I didn't know how. When I got discouraged, I thought of Katie picking up that shoe. **I would pick myself up and learn how to tie my "money shoes" into a bow for stability and growth.** I vowed to tie together the financial and emotional journey in healthy ways.

The origin of the money rascal personalities I developed later in my career goes back to this story. I love doing money personality seminars. No matter what you earn or how you feel about money, you'll discover some rejuvenating gems when you look at your money through a new lens. You'll be ready to "spring into action" and you won't have to throw anything across the room!

16

STOP Thinking

by Michael E. Gerber

Michael Gerber has spent his life understanding and improving the world of the entrepreneur. This passion led to the founding of E-Myth Worldwide in 1977 to transform the way that small business owners do the work of growing their companies. Having coached, taught and trained over 50,000 small businesses in 145 countries, Michael has become the world's preeminent small business guru. In his latest book, he shares how a conversation with his mother gave him the inspiration for his next challenge:

My mother is ninety-six, lives an active life, looks to be no more than sixty, and has a wonderful sense of humor about it all. In 2005, my mother asked me,

"SO, WHAT'S GOING ON IN YOUR LIFE, MICHAEL?"

"I'm feeling lost, Mom," I said. "I'm sixty-nine years old and I'm feeling like I used to feel when I was a kid. I don't know who I am anymore, or where I'm going. I feel disconnected from my company and disconnected from myself. I want to do something new, but I don't know what. I feel at a loss ..."

My mother said, "Michael, you've never been at a loss for ideas. You're one of the most imaginative people I know. So, we both know that it's not that you can't figure out what to do. It's that somehow you're not really dealing with the problem. Somehow you're avoiding what's really eating at you. What is it?"

I suddenly knew what it was. It came to me so quickly, so immediately, so sharply, and clearly, that I was amazed I hadn't seen it until that minute.

"I'm afraid, Mom. I'm afraid to start something brand new ... I'm afraid that I'm too old, too used up, too stuck in my E-Myth rut. And, at the same time, I'm afraid to let go of E-Myth for fear that all the work I've done, all the life I've put into it, will simply lose force and ride a slow and ugly death ..."

"Michael, the only reason you feel so conflicted is because you're coming awake to the same energy that has been bubbling and bursting and playing inside of you ever since you were a little boy. Stop thinking. It's telling you something. It's telling you that that little boy I love so much is just aching to come out. He's the one that's making such a ruckus in you. Let go, and let it do what it does. I have a feeling everything will change. It feels like it's time for something new to come into your life. Isn't that exciting?"

(Excerpted from Awakening the Entrepreneur Within.*)*

17

On Top of the Mountain

When my daughter was born, I thought it my #1 job to instill ambition and inspire greatness. But could I handle such an enormous responsibility? Raising a child calls for intelligent, life-molding decisions ... every day! I couldn't even decide on a new sofa!

So I devised a "fool-proof" strategy: read a chapter from one of my parenting how-to books before bed; brainstorm a to-do checklist for tomorrow; review the current day's checklist. Encouraged self-expression. Check. Acknowledged curiosity. Check. Reviewed ABCs. Check.

Then, one evening, everything changed.

"Everything" began in my kitchen, as I prepared dinner and my toddler lay tummy down on the kitchen floor coloring. A swirl of green over there, a whoosh of black in the middle, a thoughtful dot of brown above the black whoosh, and her work was done.

"What is it?" I asked with enthusiastic inquisitiveness, just as the child rearing books prescribed.

"IT'S ME MOMMY. I'M ON TOP OF THE MOUNTAIN."

I shared that doodle and "caption" with my own mother the next day. Without missing a beat, she said, "If only you could see how your daughter sees herself! You guided her up that mountain, and not with any of your textbooks or lists. You did it by intuition. It proves that you've got the stuff to be a great mother. **I knew that all along, but you had to figure it out for yourself. Follow your instincts and you'll do fine.**"

I framed my daughter's drawing and hung it next to my bed. I did this partly because it's a lovely drawing—once you know what it is—and partly to tickle my instincts awake every morning.

My parenting techniques took a huge leap forward once I began mixing textbook how-to with instinctive know-how. Eventually I unleashed those instincts across the board—at work, with friends, and especially when dealing with my three sisters. I had the power all along to accomplish some pretty great things ... I just had to look inside and trust what I knew. And guess what? I even bought a new sofa, which I still love, 14 years later!

18

A PUSH From Walt

In his book *How to Be Like Walt*, author Pat Williams captured the principles of Walt Disney's amazing life, from which we can all learn. Williams shared some of Walt's communications skills:

Those who worked with Walt told me again and again how approachable he was. In 1956, Walt chose renowned orchestra leader Tutti Camarata to establish Disneyland Records (now called Walt Disney Records). "Walt challenged and inspired you by talking to you," Camarata told me. "He wouldn't give you detailed instructions about what he wanted you to do. Instead, he would simply point you in the direction he wanted to go, then leave the rest up to you. He would get you started on the creative process and inspire you with confidence.

As a result, you would go far beyond what you thought you were capable of doing."

Jim Kimball, son of animator Ward Kimball and a longtime Disney employee, told me, "Walt could talk to his artists and get their juices flowing so that they could produce beyond their capabilities. He would have some wildly impossible idea, and he'd tell an artist,

"I KNOW YOU CAN DO THIS. TAKE THIS PROJECT AND GET IT DONE."

And the artist would think, "I never dreamed I could do something like that, but if Walt says I can do it, then maybe I can." And usually, Walt turned out to be right. He inspired people to do the impossible, and he did it by just talking to people.

Disney executive Orlando Ferrante has helped develop Disney theme parks around the world. He explained Walt's communication skills using sports terms. "I would list Walt Disney among the greatest coaches who ever lived. He drew up the plays, gave us our assignments, inspired us and motivated us. That's what great coaches do."

"WE KEEP MOVING FORWARD,

OPENING NEW DOORS, AND DOING NEW THINGS, BECAUSE WE'RE CURIOUS AND

CURIOSITY

LEADS US DOWN NEW PATHS."

— *Walt Disney*

19

The Daffodil PRINCIPLE

Before us lay the most glorious sight. It looked as though someone had taken a huge vat of gold and poured it down over the mountain peak and slopes. The flowers were planted in majestic, swirling patterns —great ribbons and swaths of deep orange, white, lemon yellow, salmon pink, saffron, and butter yellow.

Each different-colored variety was planted as a group so that it swirled and flowed like its own river with its own unique hue. There were five acres of flowers.

"Who has done this?" I asked my daughter.

"It's just one woman," Carolyn answered. "She lives on the property. That's her home." Carolyn pointed to a well-kept A-frame house that looked small and modest in the midst of all that glory. We walked up to the house. On the patio, we saw a poster. "Answers to the Questions I Know You Are Asking" was the headline.

The first answer was a simple one. "50,000 bulbs," it read.

The second answer was, "One at a time, by one woman. Two hands, two feet, and very little brain."

The third answer was, "Began in 1958."

There it was, The Daffodil Principle. For me, that moment was a life-changing experience. I thought of this woman whom I had never met, who, more than forty years before, had begun—one bulb at a time—to bring her vision of beauty and joy to an obscure mountaintop. Still, just planting one bulb at a time, year after year, had changed the world in which she lived.

She had created something of indescribable magnificence,beauty, and inspiration.

The principle her daffodil garden taught is one of the greatest principles of celebration. That is, learning to move toward our goals and desires one step at a time—often just one baby-step at a time—and learning to love the doing; learning to use the accumulation of time. When we multiply tiny pieces of time with small increments of daily effort, we too, will find we can accomplish magnificent things. We can change the world.

"It makes me sad in a way," I admitted to Carolyn. "What might I have accomplished if I had thought of a wonderful goal thirty-five or forty years ago and had worked away at it 'one bulb at a time' through all those years? Just think what I might have been able to achieve!"

My daughter summed up the message of the day in her usual direct way. "Start tomorrow," she said. It's so pointless to think of the lost hours of yesterdays. The way to make learning a lesson of celebration instead of a cause for regret is to ask, "What can I create and contribute today?"

(Author Unknown)

20

Good Things Happen to GOOD PEOPLE

Standing on stage with the North Park Elementary School graduating class of 2008, Principal Lynn Lawrence surveyed the 21 eighth graders and checked for a tissue in her pocket. Tonight's ceremony was destined to be a tearjerker.

This was her first graduating class to go kindergarten through eighth grade in the school's beautiful building. Oh, the school had been around for some time, opening its doors in 1980 and even earning high praise in 1998, when the *Wall Street Journal* reported, "North Park Elementary is a case study of how families and teachers working closely together can achieve surprising goals." But until 1999, this small yet mighty school functioned from two rented church basements, splitting grades K-3 and 4-8.

Recalling the "olden" days, Lynn says, "Our own building—a home— had always been a dream, but it was a high-priced dream! The emotional and financial costs were huge. I wanted to believe that we'd someday realize our dream, but I was losing hope."

By 1998, Lynn considered shelving her dream. Maybe status quo wasn't so bad after all.

That's when an incoming kindergarten dad volunteered for the school's recruiting committee. Lynn explained that this would not be an easy task. The little school garnered plenty of respect for its curriculum but lost many potential families because they functioned from church basements. People saw this as a disconnect on too many levels.

"He said to me, 'Good things happen to good people and North Park Elementary School is good people.'"

First, as an educator, I had a good chuckle over his questionable grammar. But then I realized he was right.

Lynn grabbed her dream back off the shelf and placed it—so to speak— smack in the middle of the city newspaper's real estate section. There it was. One school was moving on and their building was for sale. Within six months, North Park Elementary owned its first permanent home and

the school's enrollment almost immediately soared to an all time high.

Nine years later, Lynn clutched her tissue and addressed the 2008 graduating class, along with an auditorium filled with family and friends. "Tonight I see 21 little kindergarteners who all wanted to grow up and be important people. They believed in themselves, as did their teachers, and today they're all bright, independent thinkers, ready to move up into high school. I also see a little school housed in two disconnected church basements that wanted to grow up and be more. Someone once explained in very simple words why I should never give up on that dream. I want to pass those words on to our graduating class, and this is my story ..."

21

SKATE the Ice

In her book, *The Right Words at the Right Time*, actress and author Marlo Thomas invited one hundred remarkable people to share the moment in their life when words meant all the difference. Athlete and Olympic Champion, Scott Hamilton, shared his story:

I remember a time early in my career when I was in need of financial support to be able to continue skating. A family I had met graciously offered to sponsor my training, asking for nothing in return. Frank McLoraine was an amazing man. When I was competing at the Midwestern Sectional Championships in Chicago, I stayed at his house and I was a bundle of nerves.

He sat me down and said very simply, "Skate the ice." Those three words have stuck with me for many years, and I have applied them to many different situations. What he was telling me was to take what is given to you. Always do the best you can with what you have. I took those words to heart.

I was the only skater at the time executing a difficult triple lutz in the compulsory short program, a risky move because there are mandatory deductions for mistakes. With Mr. McLoraine's words ringing in my ears, I nailed the jump and thought to myself, "Okay, this works." I was prepared. I had done my homework and it was either going to be great or not so great. I had done everything I could so I just had to let it happen. I had to "skate the ice."

> PEOPLE LOOK AT AN EVENT LIKE THE OLYMPICS AND THINK THAT THE GOLD MEDAL IS THE ULTIMATE GOAL, BUT IT'S NOT. THE PROCESS OF GETTING THERE IS FAR MORE IMPORTANT.

I now realize that the greater results were achieved by what it took to get to that place of having the chance to succeed. It's about showing up and training with all you've got every day. It's about doing that run through when you aren't feeling well, or dragging yourself to the rink when you didn't get much sleep the night before and giving the same effort as when you're feeling your best.

THERE ARE THOSE DAYS WHEN IT'S HARD TO PUT ONE FOOT IN
FRONT OF THE OTHER, BUT THOSE ARE THE DAYS WHEN
CHAMPIONS ARE CREATED.
IT'S ABOUT MAKING THE MOST OF THE
MINUTES YOU ARE GIVEN.

22

Go for IT!

by Jack Canfield

*W*hen Debbie Macomber *decided to pursue her dream of becoming a writer, she rented a typewriter, put it on the kitchen table, and began typing each morning before the kids went to school. When the kids came home, she moved the typewriter and made them dinner. When they went to bed, she moved it back and typed some more. For two ½ years, Debbie followed this routine. Supermom had become a struggling writer and she was loving every minute of it.*

One night, however, her husband, Wayne, sat her down and said, "Honey, I'm sorry, but you're not bringing in any income. We can't do this anymore. We can't survive on just what I make."

That night, her heart broken and her mind too busy to let her sleep, she stared at the ceiling in their darkened bedroom. Debbie knew—with all of the responsibilities of keeping up a house and taking four kids to sports, church, and scouts—that working 40 hours a week would leave her no time to write.

Seeing her despair, her husband woke up and asked, "What's wrong?"

"I really think I could've made it as a writer, I really do."

Wayne was silent for a long time, then sat up, turned on the light, and said, "All right, honey, go for it."

So Debbie returned to her dream and her typewriter on the kitchen table, pounding out page after page for another two years. Her family went without vacations, pinched pennies, and wore hand-me-downs.

But the sacrifice and the persistence finally paid off. After five years of struggling, Debbie sold her first book. Then another. And another. Until finally, today, Debbie has published more than 100 books, many of which have become New York Times best-sellers and three of which have been sold for movies. Over 60 million copies of her books are in print, and she has millions of loyal fans.

And Wayne? All that sacrifice in support of his wife paid off handsomely. He got to retire at age 50 and now spends his time building an airplane in the basement of their 7,000 square-foot mansion.

Debbie's kids got a gift far more important than a few summer camps. As adults, they realize what Debbie gave them was far more important—permission and encouragement to pursue their own dreams.

(Excerpted from The Success Principles, How to Get from Where You Are to Where You Want to Be.)

"Courage is going from failure to failure without losing enthusiasm."

— *Winston Churchill*

23

Finding Your Life's
PURPOSE

by Janae Bower

Reflecting back on my life, I realize that who I've become is a reflection of the profound wisdom from those who have touched my life both briefly and deeply. However, one person and one encouraging statement is the driving force behind it all. "God has a special purpose for your life." My dad shared these words of wisdom with me many times throughout my life.

As a little girl, I felt special even though I didn't really know what these words meant. As a teenager, I was embarrassed to hear these words so I rolled my eyes and pretended they didn't matter. As a young woman, I took these words to heart. And so the search for my special purpose began.

For years, I immersed myself in books, seminars, audios and anything else that could help me find "It." Many would call my search for "It" obsessive. I call "It" finding God's special purpose for my life.

DEEP INSIDE MY HEART I FOUND THAT MY LIFE'S PURPOSE IS TO HELP OTHERS FIND

"IT",
LIVE "IT" AND GIVE "IT" AWAY.

Thirty years after first hearing my dad's words of wisdom for my destiny, I'm honoring what my dad did for me by helping others find their destiny. I started an inspirational business called Finding IT, dedicated to helping others get to the heart of what matters most, and created a free gift—a guide to help others develop their personal mission, vision and values. Most importantly as I tuck my two young boys in bed at night, I look deep into the eyes of their heart and share with them, "God has a special purpose for your life."

Spelling ~ Unit 13

1. perilous
2. vertical
3. summit
4. crevice
5. rappelling
6. descending
7. gendarme
8. mercurial
9. simultaneous
10. squall
11. Himalayas
12. stamina
13. precipitous
14. ascend
15. dissipate
16. paroxysm
17. oblivion
18. writhed
19. accelerate
20. traverse

24

C-O-N-F-I-D-E-N-C-E

by Donna Shryer

When my son Mark was eight years old, his third grade teacher announced a class spelling bee, the prize being a pizza lunch for the champ plus three friends. Mark wanted to win that contest badly. He could practically taste the pizza, hot with stringy cheese and pepperoni circles.

In honor of the spelling bee, Mark actually agreed to a haircut, and before he changed his mind, I whisked him off to the barbershop.

"Make it a lucky cut," I instructed barber Joe. "Mark's competing in a very important spelling bee next week."

"Well, did ya do your homework?" barber Joe asked.

"Yup." Mark replied.

"Did ya study hard?" barber Joe asked.

"Yup." Mark replied.

"Do ya have confidence?" barber Joe asked.

"Confidence. C-O-N-F-I-D-E-N-C-E. Confidence. A lot of people spell that one wrong," Mark explained.

"Sure. You can spell it," barber Joe responded. "But do you have it? Ya gotta have confidence in yourself, son. It's a winner's secret weapon."

Mark looked at barber Joe's reflection in the mirror, being very careful to move only his eyes and not his head for fear of losing a piece of ear to barber Joe's snipping shears. "The secret weapon, huh? Confidence!" And with that, Mark added a new catchphrase to his bag of tricks: I before e except after c; dessert has two Ss because you always want seconds; I CAN WIN THE SPELLING BEE!

And he did. And the pizza was heaven. And Mark never forgot barber Joe's words: "Ya gotta have confidence in yourself, son. It's a winner's secret weapon."

Decades later, after creating his own firm and establishing himself as a respected—albeit revolutionary—architect, Mark began receiving interview requests. Magazines loved to feature his uncanny ability to seamlessly blend cutting edge technology with old-world architectural details—sort of 1800s Painted Lady meets Dubai's 21st century Emirates Office Tower. Appropriately enough, Mark named his firm Archi-Tech.

Settling back to discuss his design approach with one particular feature writer, the reporter led with a question that almost stumped Mark. "You're considered a maverick in the world of architecture. When everyone around says it can't be done, what makes you think you can pull it off?"

After thinking a bit, Mark replied,

"Confidence. After I've done my homework, and studied my idea from every possible angle, if I still see it then I know the only thing standing between me and success is confidence. Yup, confidence. It's a winner's secret weapon."

With that, Mark swept his hand across his forehead and brushed a scruffy tuft of hair out of his eyes. "That reminds me," he said with a wink and a smile, "I need a hair cut."

25

Anonymous Angel

While comedienne and actress Carol Burnett grew up in Hollywood during the 1930s, her Hollywood was an old apartment where she lived with her grandmother, on relief, as it was called then. Her parents were divorced and both were alcoholics.

Carol attended UCLA, but knew she needed to go to New York to get a start in musical theatre. But with little money, how would she get there? In her book, *One More Time*, Carol recounts how a benefactor, who wished to remain anonymous, helped her launch her career.

"So, what do you want to do with your life?" asked Mr. C.

Carol and her boyfriend, Don, told him that they wanted to be in the theater and that New York was the only place to do it, the musical comedy capital of the world.

"Why do you want to do this?" He asked looking straight at me.

"Because I'll never be happy doing anything else."

"WHAT MAKES YOU THINK YOU'LL SUCCEED?"

"I don't think it. I know it." I amazed myself with the simplicity of the statement. I wasn't bragging. I just told him what I believed.

"Sounds to me like you two really mean it. You want this more than anything in the world. That true?"

"Yes," we both replied.

"Well, I think you might have a good shot at it. I'm gonna lend each of you a thousand dollars. You can pay it back in five years, no interest. I want you to promise to use the money to go to New York. It's enough for a ticket, and you can stretch out the rest until you find a job. Might take a little time. Tough business."

I looked down at the check. I had never seen that many zeros in my life.

We thanked him over and over and started to get up.

"Wait a minute. There are stipulations. Aside from this being a loan, you can't tell anyone my name. Also, when you do make it, you have to promise me you'll help other people out. Doesn't have to be in show business. It's up to you. Just help 'em out like I've helped you. People you think might need that one little break. Got it?"

Five years to the day, Carol repaid that loan and not only went on to become a show business legend she also became renowned for encouraging new talent along the way.

26

The Governor's Ball

My sweet son, Cameron, is 13 years old and has Rubinstein-Taybi Syndrome—a learning disability—but you can ask his teachers, friends and family and they will all tell you his heart is so full of Joy! It's a joy that he continues to share with all! He has been the most wonderful encourager, especially to me. I know his spirit is of a 100 year old soul.

Here's a story I'd like to share!

It was a beautiful red satin dress with black lace. Because of the commission position I had accepted with the state of California, **I received an invitation to Governor Arnold Schwarzenegger's Inaugural Ball.** The dress was perfect for the occasion. "Come back a few days before the ball and we'll press it for you," the store clerk said.

And so I did. But something dreadful happened. They steamed it by mistake, and the lace melted onto the satin. It was ruined, and I was crushed. I had less than 24 hours to find a new dress. With the help of the store manager and a friend, we were able to put something else together. **It was an emerald green dress and I had fancy shoes to match, though my heart yearned for my original red and black dress.**

The day was crazy. Before zooming off to the Ball, Cameron stopped me and said, "I'm sorry your dress was ruined, Mom. Your shoes are pretty, even though they are Vegas-looking shoes. The new dress is pretty, too, but remember, people are going to see your smile.

Make sure your heart and smile are connected! People will not look at your dress or shoes. They will notice your smile and the joy in your heart!"

I hugged him. He was right, it didn't matter which dress I wore. As long as I had something suitable on, I had better make sure my heart and smile were connected.

Later on in the evening, Cameron called me to ask if I was having a good time. Amused, I shared, "There are two other ladies wearing the same red and black dress!"

"Good thing you wore the green one," he laughed. **"Bet they don't have fancy Vegas shoes on!"**

Since then, whenever I am having a crazy day, he reminds me, "Hello! Your heart and smile are not connected!" He will even leave us a note taped to the front door for all of us to read before we leave: "Make sure your heart and smile are connected today, Love Cameron."

27

CONFIDENCE
of a Friend

Success is often measured by the ability to overcome adversity. But, it is often the belief of others that gives us the courage to try.

J.K. Rowling, author of the Harry Potter book series, began writing at age 6. In her biography, she remembers with great fondness when her good friend, Sean, whom she met in secondary school, became the first person to encourage her and help build the confidence that one day she would be a very good writer.

"He was the first person with whom I really discussed my serious ambition to be a writer. He was also the only person who thought I was bound to be a success at it, which meant much more to me than I ever told him at the time."

Despite many setbacks Rowling persevered in her writing, particularly fantasy stories. But it wasn't until 1990 that she first conceived the idea about Harry Potter. As she recalls, it was on a long train journey from London to Manchester when "the idea of Harry Potter simply fell into my head. To my immense frustration, I didn't have a functioning pen with me, and I was too shy to ask anybody if I could borrow one. I think, now, that this was probably a good thing, because I simply sat and thought, for four (delayed train) hours, and all the details bubbled up in my brain, and this scrawny, black-haired, bespectacled boy who didn't know he was a wizard became more and more real to me."

That same year, her mother passed away after a ten-year battle with multiple sclerosis, which deeply affected her writing. She went on to marry and had a daughter, but separated from her husband shortly afterwards.

During this time, Rowling was diagnosed with clinical depression. Unemployed, she completed her first novel in area cafes, where she could get her daughter to fall asleep. After being rejected by 12 publishing houses, the first Harry Potter novel was sold to a small British publishing house. Now with seven books that have sold nearly 400 million copies in 64 languages, J.K. Rowling is the highest earning novelist in history. And it all began with her commitment to writing that was fostered by the confidence of a friend!

(Excerpted from online biography of J.K. Rowling.)

DAVID McNALLY

As an internationally acclaimed business speaker, David McNally is among an elite group of recipients elected into the Speaker Hall of Fame by the National Speakers Association (NSA). His knowledge of what inspires people has been commended by people such as NBA coach, Pat Riley, golf superstar, Greg Norman, CNN host, Larry King, as well as hundreds of executives from many of the world's most successful companies.

David McNally is the author of two best selling books, *Even Eagles Need A Push – Learning to Soar in a Changing World* and *The Eagle's Secret – Success*

Strategies for Thriving at Work and in Life. His latest co-authored book, *Be Your OWN Brand*, demonstrates how individuals can apply the principles of brand building to develop strong personal brands. An award winning film producer, McNally has produced two highly praised, inspirational films, *The Power of Purpose* and *If I Were Brave*.

McNally's books have been translated into twelve different languages and developed into corporate training programs that have been released in over twenty countries. Abbott Laboratories, Ameriprise, Gartner Group, Merrill Lynch, Northwest Airlines, Pulte Homes, and Thrivent Financial are but a few of the many distinguished organizations that have embraced David's work as a key component of preparing their employees for an ever increasing competitive and complex future.

David McNally's mission is straightforward and clear: To provide people with the knowledge, skills and inspiration to perform at their best.

David McNally
952-835-0300
800-228-1218
www.davidmcnally.com
info@davidmcnally.com

MAC ANDERSON

Mac Anderson is the founder of Simple Truths and Successories, Inc., the leader in designing and marketing products for motivation and recognition. These companies, however, are not the first success stories for Mac. He was also the founder and CEO of McCord Travel, the largest travel company in the Midwest, and part owner/VP of sales and marketing for Orval Kent Food Company, the country's largest manufacturer of prepared salads.

His accomplishments in these unrelated industries provide some insight into his passion and leadership skills. He also brings the same passion to his speaking where he speaks to many corporate audiences on a variety of topics, including leadership, motivation, and team building.

Mac has authored or co-authored thirteen books that have sold over three million copies. His titles include:

- *Charging the Human Battery*
- *Customer Love*
- *Motivational Quotes*
- *Finding Joy*
- *You Can't Send a Duck to Eagle School*
- *212°: The Extra Degree*
- *Learning to Dance in the Rain*
- *Change is Good ... You Go First*
- *The Nature of Success*
- *The Power of Attitude*
- *The Essence of Leadership*
- *To a Child, Love is Spelled T-I-M-E*
- *The Dash*

For more information about Mac, visit www.simpletruths.com

If you have enjoyed this book we invite you to check out our entire collection of gift books, with free inspirational movies, at www.simpletruths.com. You'll discover it's a great way to inspire friends and family, or to thank your best customers and employees.

The simple truths® Difference